AF228947

CLASSIC STORIES
IN WORLD MYTHOLOGY

Don Nardo

ReferencePoint Press

San Diego, CA

For more information, contact:
ReferencePoint Press, Inc.
PO Box 27779
San Diego, CA 92198
www.ReferencePointPress.com

LIBRARY OF CONGRESS CATALOGING-IN-PUBLICATION DATA

Names: Nardo, Don, 1947- author.
Title: Classic stories in world mythology / by Don Nardo.
Description: San Diego, CA : ReferencePoint Press, Inc., 2024. | Includes
    bibliographical references and index.
Identifiers: LCCN 2023047074 (print) | LCCN 2023047075 (ebook) | ISBN
    9781678207687 (library binding) | ISBN 9781678207694 (ebook)
Subjects: LCSH: Mythology--Juvenile literature.
Classification: LCC BL312 .N37 2024 (print) | LCC BL312 (ebook) | DDC
    201/.3--dc23/eng/20231213
LC record available at https://lccn.loc.gov/2023047074
LC ebook record available at https://lccn.loc.gov/2023047075

CONTENTS

Universal Tales That Explore Life's Meaning

Mighty Zeus, leader of the Greek gods, looked down in judgment on Prometheus, deity of forethought, now bound tightly in chains. A Titan, or member of the first race of gods, Prometheus had been one of the few of his kind to back and fight for Zeus and his Olympians. Years before, the latter had defeated the Titans in a lengthy and unbelievably bloody war. And to reward Prometheus for his loyalty, Zeus had made him his chief personal adviser.

Zeus had also given the brilliant and thoughtful Titan a special task—to create a race of mortal beings who would populate the barren earth, as well as worship and provide sacrifices to the immortal gods. Prometheus had approached that chore with a great sense of purpose. He had fashioned the bodies of those small, imperfect creatures—called humans—from river mud. And in the years that followed, he had quietly watched them, frequently with pride and affection.

Over time, however, those positive feelings became increasingly tinged with worry and sadness. Prometheus saw that in winter the beings he had come to regard as his children nearly froze to death. Also, they were regularly stalked and attacked by wild animals, which they had difficulty stopping without metal weapons. Clearly, the Titan told himself, the humans desperately needed knowledge of fire so they could stay warm in winter and smelt metals to make proper weapons.

The problem was that Zeus had forbidden anyone giving fire to the humans. Let them fend for themselves, Zeus had remarked on more than one occasion. The gift of fire must remain forever a benefit to the immortals. But Prometheus, who saw this view as mean spirited, disagreed. In a daring move, he secretly stole fire from Mount Olympus, home of the gods, and gave it to the humans.

Knowledge of fire swiftly transformed human civilization. Angered by Prometheus's disobedience and by the changes he saw among the humans, Zeus ordered that Prometheus be placed in chains and secured to a large rock at the summit of a distant mountain. Thereafter, each day a giant eagle gnawed out the Titan's liver. That evening, the organ regrew. But the next day the bird returned and tore it out again, and that horrifying sequence of events repeated itself day after day, year after year.

Helping Shape Western Culture

That the moving story of Prometheus is a classic myth is nowhere disputed. Yet what makes it a classic? Put somewhat differently: what are the classic stories in mythology? Before answering that question, one must first understand what a myth is. According to the noted children's literacy organization Reading Is Fundamental, a myth is not simply an old story from past history. Indeed, a myth has little or nothing to do with history, because history consists of a factual telling of past events. Instead, says the organization,

> myths are based on religion or faith belief systems and explain natural phenomen[a], rather than tell a historical story. Many cultures have myths describing the same natural occurrences: how the world began, why the seasons change, what causes lightning or why volcanoes erupt. Myths may include supernatural beings, like Greek or Roman gods, and may include lessons about how to behave.[1]

This mention of the Greco-Roman gods is not at all surprising. In fact, in the United States, United Kingdom, France, and other

Western countries, when the word *myth* is spoken, most people think of the old Greek and Roman tales. They include, along with Prometheus's moving story, the war goddess Athena bursting from the head of her father, Zeus; the hero Perseus slaying the hideous monster Medusa; and many others. The ancient Greek myths, later borrowed by the Romans, have long pervaded and helped shape Western culture. As historians Michael Grant and John Hazel point out, "The Greek and Roman myths are an indelible, indispensable, inescapable part of our cultural background and heritage."[2]

The primary reason these stories have lasted so long can best be described as a combination of enduring social relevance

Prometheus, who is said to have created humankind, is shown stealing fire from Mount Olympus to give to the humans to provide warmth in winter and to make metal weapons to protect themselves.

and sheer quality. "These are marvelous tales," Grant and Hazel state, "which have rightly been thought worth retelling on countless thousands of occasions. As many a psychologist and anthropologist will readily confirm, they are full of profound revelations about the universal human condition and predicament." As a result of these qualities, those myths have had a profound effect on "the great and diverse fields of European art, and of European and American literature."[3]

Amazing Thematic Similarities

Despite their fame and social and artistic influence in the West, however, the Greco-Roman myths are by no means better or more important than myths from other areas of the globe. In fact, each of the world's ancient cultures produced its own myths. Moreover, more often than not the non-Western mythologies feature characters, situations, and themes that are amazingly similar to those in the Greek tales. In the words of historian Joshua J. Mark, the Greek myth of Prometheus, the fire-bringer, "is echoed in the Chinese tale of Fuxi [the god of fire]."[4] Similarly, he says, elements of the Greek creation tale can be found in the creation myths of China, Central America, Mesopotamia (now Iraq), India, and elsewhere.

Whatever the theme may be, Mark adds, the parallels among world myths abound. "African myth," he points out, "Native American myth, Chinese, or European, all serve the same function of explaining, comforting, and providing meaning." It is precisely this universality of certain tales in each culture, along with their power to make people think and act in various ways, that makes them classic. Each individual who reads or hears such stories, regardless of where in the world the stories originated, recognizes something innately relevant and important in them. Thus, says Mark, the world's classic myths "still resonate with a modern audience precisely because the ancient writers crafted them toward individual interpretation, leaving each person who heard the story to recognize the meaning in the tale for themselves and respond to it accordingly."[5]

CHAPTER ONE

Stories of Creation

One of the four main creation myths held sacred by the ancient Egyptians was one championed by the priests at Thebes. That city was Egypt's capital during what modern experts have dubbed the New Kingdom (lasting from 1550 to 1069 BCE). According to the priests, two primeval and powerful gods were responsible for creating the world, plants, animals, and human beings.

One of those creator deities was Amun, who the priests said had a sort of dual personality. First he was a member of the Ogdoad, a group of eight very ancient gods who floated in a vast, dark sea that long ago made up the whole universe. In addition to his role as one of those eight floating deities, however, Amun was secretly something much greater. Namely, he was the almighty Amun-Ra, supreme god of all that exists. Thanks to his limitless powers, he was able to absorb the other seven members of the Ogdoad. Thereafter, he felt compelled to indulge in a huge, vigorous burst of creation, in the process making dry land, mountains, lakes, plants, and the thousands of species of animals that inhabit nature.

For reasons still unknown, one important job that Amun-Ra did not undertake was the creation of humanity. That crucial task he left to his highly industrious and talented fellow deity Khnum. Depicted by Egyptian artists as having a ram's head atop a man's muscular body, Khnum oversaw the Nile River's annual floods. But in the eyes of posterity, his most memorable achievement was fashioning people from the special clay found only along the Nile's banks. Khnum was said to have sat quietly at a big potter's wheel and methodically molded each human body one at a time. Then he added hearts, lungs, and other organs to them and breathed into their mouths, an action that made them come to life.

In some parts of Egypt, people passed along a very ancient myth about Khnum that pictured him as a sort of universal creator much like Amun-Ra, as well as the controller of the enormous flow of the Nile's waters. Because those waters made agriculture possible in Egypt's otherwise dry environment, Khnum could either *cause* a drought or *alleviate* one. A surviving inscription tells how, during a widespread drought-driven famine, Khnum came to the reigning Egyptian king in a dream and said, "I am Khnum, your creator. . . . I am master of creation [and] I will make the Nile swell for you . . . so the plants will flourish. . . . The land of Egypt is beginning to stir again, the shores are shining wonderfully, and wealth and well-being dwell with them, as it had been before."[6]

A Fascination for Beginnings

That the ancient Egyptians recognized multiple creation stories and creator gods clearly demonstrates their powerful preoccupation with the origins of the world and everything contained within it, including people. Moreover, they were far from alone in this fascination for understanding the beginnings of things. Indeed, anthropologist Robert L. Carneiro points out, the origins of the universe and humanity are "among the most basic questions raised by human beings." All around the world, he goes on, early societies wondered, "How did the human species arise? How was the Earth created? What about the sun? the moon? the stars?" For ancient cultures everywhere, it seemed only logical that "people and the world exist because they were brought into being by a series of creative acts. Moreover, this creation is usually regarded as the work of supernatural beings or forces."[7]

Although most of the cultures that believed in the existence of such creator deities vanished long ago, a good many of the tales of those supernatural beings have survived. Unquestionably, one

of the more intriguing aspects of those surviving creation myths is that, despite emerging from places thousands of miles apart, most share certain basic ideas, plots, and themes. Common, for instance, is the notion that in the beginning there was only a vast, dark, swirling sea or a dark, spinning mixture of chaotic elements. And out of that fluid, murky mass, one or more primordial, supernatural beings emerged.

From Darkness and Chaos to Light and Order

In fact, that is exactly how the early Greeks, very much like the ancient Egyptians, pictured the creation. The Greeks called the universe—consisting of everything that exists—the cosmos. The sixth-century-BCE Greek epic poet Hesiod wrote that at first the cosmos was composed of a dark, spinning, disorganized assemblage of unidentified substances. He and other Greek thinkers called it Chaos. According to the late classical scholar W.H.D. Rouse, within that scrambled concoction drifted "the seeds or beginnings of all things [all] mixed up together in a shapeless mass, all moving about in all directions."[8]

Seemingly countless centuries elapsed, during which nothing changed. But then, in an unforeseen turn of events, two shapeless living beings leaped into existence. Those two lumps of consciousness—Night and Erebus—became aware of their surroundings and each other, and they mated almost immediately. The result was an egg that grew within Erebus's formless body.

More time passed, and when the egg finally burst open, out flew a truly miraculous being whom the Greeks came to call Eros, meaning "love." Sometimes they referred to him as "God." Whatever he was called, he produced an immense torrent of pure light that suddenly flooded outward, erasing the darkness and turning disorder into order. In the words of the Roman storyteller Ovid, "God unlocked all elemental things." The lighter elements floated upward and became the sky, while the heavier ones sank downward, forming the land. And, said Ovid, "at God's touch lakes, springs, dancing waterfalls streamed downhill into valleys, waters glancing through rocks, grass, and wild-flowered meadows."[9]

Indeed, across Earth's surface, plants and animals sprang into being. The Greeks did not envision Eros himself creating these things, as if by magic. Instead, they viewed him as a great organizer. The general belief was that the seeds of rocks, trees, mountains, flowers, and animals had already existed within Chaos and that Eros was somehow able to release them in an ordered way.

A Being with an Amazing Work Ethic

The fact that multiple supernatural beings were involved in various aspects of both the Egyptian and Greek visions of the creation is no coincidence. Similar situations appear in the creation myths

The Greeks' Grandmother

The chief ancient Greek creation myth suggests that no single god created the universe and other conscious beings. Rather, the cosmos had already long existed in a state of chaos, perhaps for an infinite amount of time. At some point in the dim past, several divine beings, including Eros, appeared from out of that chaotic state. Not long after he hatched from an egg and brought light to the darkness, two of the most important of all the Greek divinities arose. One was Gaia, or Mother Earth, a gigantic consciousness embodying the planet itself. The other vast being was Uranus, or Father Heaven, personifying the sky. According to the surviving myths, those two beings mated several times, in each case creating a new brood of offspring. At first they produced only misshapen monsters, including several one-eyed giants (the Cyclopes). Later, however, Gaia and Uranus gave birth to the first race of gods, the large, physically perfect, and very powerful Titans. Partly because the kindly Titan Prometheus fashioned humans from river mud or clay, the Greeks thought of Gaia as, in a sense, the grandmother of their own race, and people commonly prayed to her for guidance or luck.

of many past peoples around the globe. In ancient China, for example, two gods equivalent in several ways to Egypt's Amun and Khnum were thought to be responsible for fashioning the world and humanity. The first of the two Chinese creator deities was Pangu. Like Egypt's Amun and Greece's Eros, he came into being within a seemingly limitless expanse of darkness and swirling forces.

Also, as Eros supposedly did, Pangu emerged from a long period of gestation inside a big egg. No one has ever known where Pangu's egg originated. More certain, at least according to the third-century-CE Chinese writer Xu Zheng, was that Pangu remained inside that object, fast asleep, for eighteen thousand years. When the creator finally woke up, he was unhappy to find himself enveloped in darkness. So he wished for an ax to appear in his right hand, and the object magically materialized. Pangu used that tool to chop at the surrounding layers of shell, and in the words of the myth teller for the Chinese ballet company Shen Yun, "the egg split into two with a thunderous crack."[10]

The liberated Pangu was blessed with what might be called an amazingly strong and effective work ethic. Wasting no time, mere seconds after emerging from the primordial egg, he employed his ax to begin breaking up the remaining slabs of shell. The lighter pieces floated upward and formed the sky, while the heavier pieces sank downward and became Earth's solid surface. After working diligently for several thousand more years, Pangu was so exhausted that he laid down and died. Yet the remains of his immense body aided in further acts of miraculous creation. His final breath became the clouds in the sky, for instance, and the last echoes of his booming voice became the first thunder. Moreover, the Shen Yun storyteller adds, Pangu's "left eye blazed into the sun and right eye gleamed into the moon; his hair and beard became stars of the Milky Way; his limbs and hands and feet

This eighteenth-century print shows Pangu holding the cosmic egg that he emerged from. After emerging, he immediately started working to create the sky and the earth.

transformed into great mountains and the blood running through his veins into flowing rivers."[11]

One vital aspect of the world that Pangu did not make was human beings. That task fell to a later creator deity named Nuwa. A few centuries after Pangu's passing, Nuwa suddenly appeared in the sky. Although she was highly impressed with Pangu's work, she felt that something was missing. A race of mortal beings who could farm the land and fish in the seas would give the world purpose, she decided. So, using the nutrient-rich, yellow-colored silt lining the banks of the Yellow River, she fashioned humans.

The Beginning of a Tragic End?

The idea that Pangu created the world and Nuwa made humans is fairly simple and straightforward and was therefore easy for average people in ancient China to grasp and accept. The situation was similar in Egypt, with Amun creating earth and the heavens and Khnum fashioning people. Likewise, most ancient societies and religions featured two or three deities who shared the individual tasks involved in the creation. The Jews, Christians, and

The Aztec Ark

Most people today do not realize that one of the several creation myths of the Aztecs, whose empire once spanned large portions of what is now Mexico, closely resembles the renowned biblical story about the great flood, Noah, and the ark. The Aztec version takes place near the end of the Fourth Sun, one of the five worlds created by the early Aztec gods. In the myth, the deity Tezcatlipoca approaches a human man and woman—Nata and Nena—and informs them that a giant flood will soon engulf the known world. The god advises the couple to build a big boat from cypress wood in hopes of riding out and surviving the disaster. Nata and Nena proceed to construct the vessel, finishing it mere days before the deluge begins. Safe on the ship, the two manage to survive the flood, and after the water subsides, they catch and eat some fish to alleviate their hunger. Suddenly, Tezcatlipoca reappears and reprimands them for eating the fish. This was wrong, he explains, because during the flood some gods had turned the other people into fish, which means that the couple had engaged in cannibalism. As a punishment, he transforms them into dogs.

Muslims, who envision a single divine creator, are well-known exceptions to that rule.

Another exception—one that remains almost unique in the annals of world mythology—is the case of the Aztecs, who built an impressive empire in southern Mexico during the 1400s and 1500s. They envisioned the creation as highly complex. In their view numerous gods and even several separate races of people were involved at different stages.

Moreover, the first of those creator deities was physically unlike practically every other god in the world's collected myths. Its name was Ometeotl, and a number of modern historians think it possessed dual genders, so that it was both a "he" and a "she." A description of this confluence of conflicting characteristics in a single deity appears in an ancient Aztec song, which goes in part, "He/She is the star which illumines all things and he/she is the Lady of the shining skirt of stars. He/She is our mother [and] our father."[12]

The line about Ometeotl being the mother and father of the gods is a literal reference to the fact that he/she supposedly mated with himself/herself, producing four sons. Those four gods then went on a veritable creation spree that lasted thousands of years. During that span, five separate creations occurred, each generating a unique world the Aztecs called a "sun." Each was overseen by a different deity and featured a race of humans created by that god. Also, each of the first four suns ended in a major natural catastrophe. The Aztecs themselves believed that they were living in the Fifth Sun and assumed that someday their world would be destroyed too.

That the Aztecs completely accepted the myths that told how each of their five worlds was divinely created demonstrates a belief they shared with ancient societies around the globe. Most members of all those cultures felt strongly that the tales of those beginnings had the ring of truth. In large part, this was because ancient societies had little or no sense of history or progress. They did not conceive of human culture becoming progressively more advanced over time, as is common today. According to the late scholar H.W.F. Saggs, they assumed the world had changed little or not at all since a god or gods had created it long before. "With no concept of social progress," he wrote, "they had no incentive to make a conscious record of life in the thousands of years before."[13] Indeed, there seemed no need to do so, since the future was expected to be little different than the past. Thus, they typically fell back on their existing myths, and always central to those stories were the ones that told how the gods, world, and people had originated.

CHAPTER TWO

Stories of Warring Gods

Apsu, the regal Babylonian god of fresh water, sat on his golden throne and pressed his hands to the sides of his head. This must be the worst headache he had ever endured, he said to himself. Hoping to end his torment, he summoned his close confidante, Tiamat, goddess of salt water. When she asked Apsu what ailed him, he explained that the many other deities who oversaw the world and humanity were constantly chattering on and on about multiple topics and thereby creating an infernal racket. And therefore he had a splitting headache. As set down in the surviving Babylonian epic known as the *Enuma Elish*, he told her, "Their behavior has become displeasing to me, and I cannot rest in the day-time or sleep at night. I will destroy and break up their way of life, [in order] that silence may reign."[14]

Tiamat responded that the loud din Apsu described had been bothering her as well. She offered to unleash the hideous, hungry serpents that swam in her seas, which would swallow and eliminate most of those noisy deities. Before Apsu and Tiamat could launch their assault, however, Ea, Apsu's grandson and god of wisdom, got wind of the plot. The younger deity warned Tiamat to desist, but she took his cautionary advice as an insult and decided to destroy him before launching the larger attack. She called forth her vicious serpents, along with numerous other vile creatures, among them (according to the *Enuma Elish*) "fierce demons, the Fish-man, and the Bull-man . . . fearless in the face of battle."[15]

When Ea beheld this array of monstrous beings, he realized there was only one chance to save himself and his fellow deities. He must enlist the aid of the most powerful living being in existence—his son Marduk. For reasons that no one could explain, the young god was already stronger than all the other deities combined; moreover, the child possessed uncanny courage and fighting skills.

When Ea asked Marduk for help, the son smiled and told his father not to worry. Donning battle armor, the young god drove

Marduk is pictured here, driving his father's chariot in pursuit of Tiamat.

his dad's chariot out on the open plain where the repulsive ones had gathered. In the fierce battle that followed, the valiant Marduk accomplished a stunning victory. He pursued the fast-fleeing monsters and one by one sliced them to pieces. Finally, he caught up to the now terrified Tiamat, and as recorded in the *Enuma Elish*, "with his merciless club [he] smashed her skull [and] severed her arteries."[16] Thereafter, the Babylonians recognized Marduk as the king of heaven and worshipped him with all due respect and reverence.

Real Rather than Mere Fable?

The short but decisive war among the Babylonian supernatural beings was by no means an uncommon occurrence in the annals of the world's numerous national mythologies. Quite literally, dozens of ancient peoples around the globe recorded in their religious literature various heavenly battles or wars said to have taken place in the dim past. Those peoples included the Japanese in eastern Asia, the Hindus in India, the Aztecs in Mexico, and many others. "These battles have become the stuff of legend," says noted Indian filmmaker Shashank, "forever etched in the annals of history as tales of bravery, power, and sacrifice." He adds, "These stories continue to inspire and intrigue us to this day."[17]

The Hindu heavenly war, starring the famous hero Rama, is particularly inspiring to millions of people today because most modern Indians are convinced it is not merely a legend or fable from a long-ago world. Rather, the vast majority of Hindus believe that Rama actually *is* an avatar, or manifestation, of the "preserver" god Vishnu (himself an avatar of the sole god, Brahman). Furthermore, they hold that his epic fight against an army of demons was an actual event.

This exciting story, chronicled in the great Hindu epic the *Ramayana*, begins untold thousands of years ago. In that remote

Rama's First Victory

In the Hindu epic the *Ramayana*, before kidnapping Rama's wife, the demon king Ravana launched a preliminary attack on Rama, whose forces had not yet fully formed. Putting one of his demon generals in charge of the attack force, Ravana ordered that minion to kill Rama and all his officers. Fortunately for Rama, however, his scouts spotted the approaching demon horde, giving him some needed time to prepare. Donning his armor, wrought of gold mixed with iron, he stood on a low hill situated right in the path of the oncoming enemy. At the demon general's order, his archers sent their arrows flying at the lone figure in the distance. But as the *Ramayana* says, employing his shield with blinding speed, the avatar of mighty Vishnu deftly deflected those incoming shafts. Then it was his turn. He returned fire in a massive, lightning-fast volley, producing a barrage of hundreds of arrows that each sought out its foe, "piercing its heart." Shrieking loudly, the demons fell, "like dry wood consumed by fire. Again and again Rama [bends] his bow like a sickle, sending forth the deadly arrows that [seem] to darken the sun." The demon general was among the dead.

Hari P. Shastri, trans., *Ramayana*, ed. Elizabeth Seeger. New York: Scott, 1969, p. 106.

era, Ravana, the huge and evil king of the demon kingdom of Lanka, grew increasingly angry. He and his demonic military generals had long desired to attack and destroy the Hindu gods and their human allies. In particular, the demonic elite wanted to achieve vengeance on Rama, who over time had killed large numbers of demons.

The Strongest Force in the World

In preparation for his attack on Rama and the gods, Ravana boarded his flying chariot. Soaring through the sky, he traveled to the castle of one of his leading followers—a demon named Marich. According to a modern retelling of the *Ramayana*, Ravana shouted, "You must help me destroy this Rama and obtain his wife Sita for me."[18]

At first Marich was reluctant to get involved because he seriously feared Rama. No one could defeat that hero, he told Ravana. The latter grabbed him by the throat and hissed, "How dare you contradict me? It is your place to obey. Now do as I say or I will kill you."[19] Not surprisingly, the frightened Marich did as his king commanded. He kidnapped Rama's beloved wife, Sita, took her to Lanka, and threw her into a grimy prison cell.

When Rama discovered what had happened, he leaped into action. He contacted his half brother, Lakshmana, and the two quickly raised an army of gods and humans. Upon arriving in the demon king's realm, Rama and his soldiers engaged in furious combat with the dark demonic forces. The battle went on for hours, until most of the demons were either slain or fleeing for their lives.

Desperate to destroy his enemy, Ravana challenged Rama to fight him in single combat. Accepting, Rama ran straight toward the demon king. "Both knew all the science of warfare," the *Ramayana* states, "and neither had ever known defeat. Each sent forth a cloud of arrows as they circled about each other."[20]

Rama and Lakshmana fight against Ravana. This Hindu heavenly war is one of many heavenly wars said to have taken place.

In time, the ghastly demon grew increasingly fatigued and finally collapsed in a heap, which allowed Rama to slay him. Less than an hour later, Rama was reunited with his wife. She had been certain all along that he would come and rescue her, she told him, for he was the purest possible representation of the strongest force in the world—goodness.

Earth's Surface Devastated

While goodness with its perpetual opposition to evil was the ideal that drove the heavenly Hindu war, the famous conflict among the Greek gods was driven by a very different theme—the acquisition of naked power. The first race of gods—the Titans—had run the world for a long time. But after Cronos, their leader, badly misused his own children, they turned on him. Led by Zeus, his sister Hera, and his brothers Hades and Poseidon, the members of that angry brood prepared for a battle to end all battles.

Because Zeus's forces were badly outnumbered, he convinced some of the more sympathetic Titans to join him. Prominent among those allies were Prometheus, who could foresee future events; his brother, Epimetheus; and their mother, Themis. Prometheus later remembered (according to the Greek playwright Aeschylus, in his play *Prometheus Bound*), "My mother had many times foretold to me that not brute strength, not violence, but instead cunning must give victory to the rulers of the future. This I explained to [the warmongering Titans], which they found not worth one moment's heed. Then, of the courses open to me, it seemed best to take my stand—my mother with me—at the side of Zeus."[21]

After the two sides had made their war preparations, the floodgates of remorseless combat opened. Each of the opposing armies, made up of immortal beings who could not be killed by ordinary means, set out to exhaust, capture, and imprison the other. Day after day the combatants raged against one another in what the later Greeks called the Titanomachy, or War of the Titans. In that mighty struggle, no thought was given to preserving the intricacy and beauty of Earth's surface. Members of both

Hesiod Describes the War in Heaven

The first important writer to describe the Titanomachy—the war between the Titans and Olympians—was Hesiod. Along with Homer, he was one of the two greatest early Greek epic poets. Because no accurate historical records were kept in their era, no one knows for sure when Hesiod was born. But the educated guess of modern experts places the date sometime in the late 700s or early 600s BCE. He made his living primarily as a well-to-do farmer in Boeotia, the region of central Greece subject to Thebes. Like his brother, Perses, he also acted as a legal adviser for some of his neighbors. The only reason that these and other facts about Hesiod are known is that he stated them in the texts of his short epic poems, the *Works and Days* and the *Theogony*. The latter, roughly translated as "the lineage of the gods," primarily cites the early Greek creation myths. In fair detail, Hesiod described how Creation developed out of the swirling elements of Chaos; the appearance of Gaia, or Mother Earth; the rise of the Titans; and the rebellion of Zeus and his divine siblings.

sides regularly uprooted large trees to use as clubs and drowned lush valleys under towering sea waves. In the words of the Greek epic poet Hesiod, "The boundless sea rang terribly around and the Earth crashed loudly. Wide Heaven was shaken and groaned, and high [Mount] Olympus reeled from its foundation under the charge of the undying gods."[22]

The shamelessly destructive war continued for years, until finally the tide turned in favor of Zeus and his followers. They steadily prevailed over their opponents, and Cronos and his own followers had no choice but to surrender. Bound in chains, they were confined to dismal Tartarus (the underworld's lowest layer) for eternity. The victors, meanwhile, took charge of the world and started rebuilding it. They also erected several magnificent palaces atop Mount Olympus and thereafter, appropriately, became known as the Olympian gods.

The Universe in Ruins

The ancient Greeks assumed that the Olympian gods not only were real but also would be around to oversee the world virtually forever. Furthermore, that was a supposition routinely made by the vast majority of ancient peoples around the world about their own deities. There was a singular exception to that rule, however—that of the Norse (often called the Vikings), who initially inhabited Scandinavia and later other parts of Europe.

Like many other peoples in history, the Norse envisioned in their myths a major war involving the gods and other supernatural forces. What made the Norse version highly unusual was its tragic outcome, which had been forecast in an ancient prophecy. That prediction had warned that there would eventually be a huge, climactic battle called Ragnarok, or the Twilight of the Gods. It would be a struggle between the Norse gods, aided by their human allies, and a coalition of evil beings and monsters. Most crucially, and disturbingly, the prophecy stated, the evil ones would be victorious.

One might suppose that the Norse deities would simply admit defeat and not bother to engage in a losing fight. Yet the opposite was true. In a phenomenally heroic display, the gods opted to fight on till their last breaths. In the words of the late, great modern mythologist Edith Hamilton, in the face of inevitable doom, knowing full well their cause is hopeless, "the gods will fight for it to the end. . . . They know that they cannot save themselves . . . [but] even so, they [will] not yield. They [will] die resisting."[23]

As Ragnarok approached, within the formidable group of creatures arrayed against the gods were numerous giants. Said to be eaters of human flesh, they hated the gods. Allied to them were the monstrous offspring of the trickster god, Loki, who treacherously betrayed his fellow deities. Among his savage children were Jormungandr, a gigantic, perpetually hungry serpent; and an equally huge and dangerous wolf named Fenrir.

On the day of the great battle, these and hundreds of other malevolent beings converged on Asgard, realm of the gods. The latter donned their armor and resolutely marched out to meet the

This painting depicts Ragnarok, a battle between gods and evil beings that was predicted in Norse mythology. The serpent Jormungandr, and the wolf, Fenrir, are shown.

foe. As the forces of good and evil clashed in the hours that followed, the entire world shook; the ground rose and fell like ocean waves; the fearful stars retreated from the sky; and towering mountains crumbled, crushing whole cities.

In the awful turmoil, the gods fought with unmatched skill and courage. These "champions of men," expert on the Norse Daniel McCoy writes, fought "more valiantly than anyone [had] ever fought before. But it [was] not enough."[24] As the wondrous deities perished, the universe creaked and sagged and fell into wretched ruin, leaving the few surviving giants and monsters crawling like maggots through the wreckage.

Many Norse feared that this predicted vision of Ragnarok would indeed someday come to pass. Others, however, refused to accept such a hopeless future. These optimists passed on a more positive alternative story in which a few gods and humans would survive the final battle and in time rebuild the devastated world. Whichever of these myths they accepted, all Vikings readily agreed that the gods were good, honorable beings who had created and long protected humanity. Moreover, a similar belief formed the core of the god worship practiced by the Hindus, Greeks, and all other devout past peoples. This divine vision, said the late scholar H.R.E. Davidson, "is a noble one. The gods are heroic figures, humans writ large, who . . . [possess] a firm sense of values. . . . We find in [their] myths [a] spirit of heroic resignation . . . [acceptance that] courage, adventure, and the wonders of life are matters for thankfulness, to be enjoyed while life is still granted to us."[25]

CHAPTER THREE

Stories of Epic Quests

One day long, long ago, the chief Norse deity, Odin, decided to embark on his next quest for knowledge, especially about nature's most hidden secrets and workings. He had undertaken several such journeys over the course of the preceding ages, and each had allowed him to store some new and enlightening facts in his vast, mazelike intellect. In fact, next to his duties as leader of the gods, he was most often preoccupied with collecting knowledge.

This particular quest was the most important yet for Odin. He had long heard that a certain very secretive supernatural being named Mimir had stored many of the universe's most innermost secrets in a magical pond called Mímisbrunnr, or Mimir's Well. It was said one could acquire that precious knowledge by drinking from that pond. However, it was necessary to obtain Mimir's express permission first.

After several months of relentless searching, Odin had finally located the dark grotto in which the mystical well was located. Stepping out of the sunlight and into the shade of the grotto's overhanging trees, he slowly and cautiously approached the well. A few seconds later, the massive face of a man materialized in the rocks on the far side of the pool. Clearly, Odin reasoned, this must be the legendary Mimir.

The two extraordinary beings contemplated each other for quite some time. Then Odin introduced himself. Mimir replied that the introduction was unnecessary, for he knew full well he was addressing the leader of the Norse gods. Odin politely asked if it was all right to drink from the pond, to which Mimir said yes, but only on one condition. Namely, Odin would need to pay a sort of toll, in the form of a major personal sacrifice. Specifically, in Odin's case, Mimir said, the god would have to toss one of his own eyes into the pool.

This was an extraordinarily stiff price to pay, Odin realized. But he felt it would be worth it if doing so meant he could absorb the tantalizing store of knowledge in the water before him. Odin removed a knife from his belt, raised it up before his face, and after taking a deep breath, swiftly scooped out his right eye. Then he threw it into Mímisbrunnr's dark waters.

Mimir wasted no time in keeping his side of the grim bargain. Filling a drinking horn with liquid from the pond, he handed it to the now one-eyed god, who sipped from it immediately. Feeling a stream of new facts flowing into his mind, Odin considered that his newest quest had been successful, and he smiled at the realization that he was now the wisest single being in existence.

Odin is pictured at the magical pond known as Mimir's Well, where he was forced to give up his eye so that he could drink.

From Bully to Model Ruler

Epic quests for adventure, treasure, secret knowledge, and other assorted prizes have been an ever-present feature of human mythology and literature throughout the ages. Of the many examples from ancient cultures, a few stand out as iconic and are still told and retold in novels, paintings, sculptures, and most recently films and video games. Besides Odin's quests for knowledge, perhaps the most famous are the Mesopotamian hero Gilgamesh's search for the secret of immortality, the Greek hero Jason's quest to capture the magical Golden Fleece, and the Roman hero Aeneas's search for a new homeland.

As for why such stories continue to fascinate people in each new generation, undoubtedly it is partly because they are so entertaining. In addition, some mythologists speculate, new portrayals of such tales provide ordinary people an indirect way to take part in exotic adventures they will never experience in real life. For example, everyone knows that human beings cannot live forever. But Gilgamesh's search for eternal life can still excite people to imagine or wish such a thing could be true.

His famous tale first emerged in the 4000s BCE in Mesopotamia, what is now Iraq. At first he was far from a hero. Though king of the city of Uruk and a skilled warrior, he was an arrogant and loudmouthed bully. Fed up with his bad behavior, the local elders asked Aruru, the goddess who protected the town, for help. She fashioned an artificial man named Enkidu from clay. At first he was wild and untamed and lived in the forest like a beast. Hearing about him, Gilgamesh brought him into the local palace and made a show of trying to civilize him. This played right into Aruru's hands, for she made sure that Enkidu became more civilized and well-mannered than Gilgamesh himself.

Nevertheless, Gilgamesh liked Enkidu, and the two became friends. Moreover, following the example of Enkidu's decent qualities, Gilgamesh saw the error of his own former ways and became a model ruler loved by his people. In the months that followed,

Gilgamesh and his best friend did as many good deeds as they could and helped dozens of people in a variety of ways.

A Monumental Truth

Eventually, however, Gilgamesh and Enkidu became involved in a far less positive situation. Ishtar, goddess of love, demanded that Gilgamesh marry her. When he refused (because he did not feel he was ready for marriage), she caused Enkidu to fall ill and die. Prostrate with grief, Gilgamesh told the elders, "I must weep for Enkidu, my friend, and mourn bitterly."[26]

Not long thereafter, Gilgamesh suddenly realized what he could do to honor the memory of his lost friend. He would search for a way to defeat death. Thus, he made it his life's mission to find the secret of immortality, not only for himself but also for people everywhere.

This great quest took the young man far and wide. Eventually, he heard a rumor that a king named Utnapishtim knew where to find the secret of eternal life. That ruler dwelled far to the west on an island in a great sea. After overcoming several difficulties, Gilgamesh made it to the island and entered Utnapishtim's man-

Ea's Timely Warning

Before the old man revealed the location of the flower that granted eternal life, he told Gilgamesh the story of how, many years before, the gods created a catastrophic worldwide flood. Fortunately for Utnapishtim, the god Ea had warned him about the coming disaster and had advised him to construct a big boat. Place a few people aboard it, Ea had said, and as many animals as he could fit. Utnapishtim had taken that advice. In the boat, he and his passengers rode out the deluge, which killed millions of people and animals. After seven days, the waters subsided and Utnapishtim witnessed the desolation the gods had brought about. "Silence reigned," he told Gilgamesh (in the text of the ancient document *The Epic of Gilgamesh*), "for all of humanity had returned to clay [become lifeless and formless]. The flood-plain was as flat as a roof. I opened a porthole and light fell on my cheeks. I bent down, then sat. I wept. My tears ran down my cheeks."

Quoted in Stephanie Dalley, trans., *Myths from Mesopotamia*. New York: Oxford University Press, 1989, pp. 113–14.

sion. There, the older man told him that he had long ago survived a great flood that covered the world's surface. And because he saved a few people and animals in a boat he had built, a god had rewarded him by revealing the source of immortality.

That source, Utnapishtim told Gilgamesh, was a plant called the flower of youth, which would give eternal life to anyone who tasted it. It grew at the bottom of the sea nearby, he added. Excited at this news, Gilgamesh dove into the water and managed to retrieve the magical flower. After that, he set out for home, intending to allow his people to benefit from that wonderful gift. Months elapsed. And when he was only a few miles from Uruk, he stopped to rest and fell asleep. When he awakened, he witnessed a snake take the flower and escape with it. Although Gilgamesh's quest had ultimately failed, it had taught him one of life's monumental truths. Namely, only the gods are immortal, whereas humans, no matter how good or powerful, must all face death in the end.

Voyage of the Argo

A magical object of a different kind was involved in the hero Jason's renowned quest. He set out to find the Golden Fleece, the hide of a magical ram that had the power to heal a person of any illness. The epic voyage to Colchis, a distant land on the shores of the Black Sea, where the fleece was said to rest, required much preparation. Jason first enlisted the aid of the master shipbuilder Argus, who swiftly constructed a large, sturdy vessel that he dubbed the *Argo*, after himself. For the crew, who appropriately became known as the Argonauts, Jason enlisted several of the strongest, most skilled, and noblest men of Greece. Among them were the mighty strongman Heracles (today better known as Hercules); the master musician and brave warrior Orpheus; and Castor and Polydeuces, twin sons of the god Zeus.

When the ship was ready, the Argonauts sailed north, bound for the Black Sea's little-known waters. Along the way they encountered and managed to overcome numerous dangerous obstacles. One consisted of making it through a channel bordered by the dreaded Clashing Rocks. When the rocks detected an incoming ship, they compressed inward and crushed the vessel into a pile of splinters. In another hair-raising episode, Jason and his men encountered and subdued the Harpies, terrifying flying creatures with razor-sharp claws and a sickening stench.

Finally, the ship made it to Colchis, where the local king, Aeëtes, had control of the legendary Golden Fleece. Because Aeëtes distrusted foreigners, when Jason asked for the fleece, the king refused and then hatched a plot to kill the chief Argonaut. Jason had to fight a dragon and an army of seed warriors, powerful fighters who grew from dragons' teeth planted in the ground. Meanwhile, Aeëtes's daughter, Medea, who was a sorceress, had fallen in love with Jason at first sight. After his victory over the seed warriors, she helped him steal the fleece, and the Argonauts escaped and sailed back to Greece with their prize.

Jason had to fight a dragon in order to steal the Golden Fleece, which had the power to heal a person of any illness.

What the Gods Foresaw

The Argonauts' great adventure was said to have taken place in the generation just preceding the Trojan War. In that famous conflict, a coalition of Greek kings besieged and sacked the rich trading city of Troy, in what is now northwestern Turkey. A number of renowned warriors fought in the war, including the legendary Greek fighter, Achilles, and the great Trojan champion, Hector. The latter, son of the Trojan king, and most of Troy's other princes and leaders died in the fighting.

The lone exception was Aeneas, Hector's brother. Aeneas and some followers escaped in a few ships and began to search for a new home. They sailed southwest into the Aegean Sea and stopped momentarily on a small island. There they unexpectedly received a message from Apollo, god of prophecy. According to the Roman writer Virgil in his epic, the *Aeneid*, Apollo told Aeneas, "There is a place the Greeks have called Hesperia—the western land. [It is] an ancient country powerful in war and rich of soil. The inhabitants call themselves Italians . . . [and] there lies your true home."[27]

Although Aeneas and his companions had no way of knowing the outcome, they chose to follow the god's advice and continued sailing westward.

The Power of Selected Myths

After experiencing a number of exciting and at times dangerous adventures, Aeneas and his followers finally made landfall on Italy's western coast. There Aeneas encountered a mysterious sorceress known as the Sibyl, who took him into a cave that led downward to the edge of the dark underworld. There Aeneas met with the shade, or soul, of his father, Anchises, who had recently died. Anchises eagerly conjured up for his son a vision of the future. "I shall show you the whole span of our destiny," he told Aeneas. Their descendants would build a town called Alba Longa, and the line of its rulers would lead to a man named Romulus. It would be Romulus, Anchises explained, who would found history's most important city—Rome. "Our glorious Rome," he stated with pride, "shall rule the whole wide world, and her spirit shall match the spirit of the gods."[28]

After returning to the surface, Aeneas sailed farther north, to the Latium Plain, where he and his people traveled down the Tiber River. A few weeks later they met and allied themselves with the local Italians, and in time Aeneas married the daughter of the region's king.

High up above, mighty Jupiter looked down approvingly on the unfolding series of events. In the centuries that followed, the former Trojans merged with the Italians, creating a new and ex-

Aeneas is pictured (in the gaping mouth of a great demon) being taken to the underworld by Sibyl. While there, he met the soul of his dead father and saw a vision of the future.

The Classic Telling of Aeneas's Quest

By far the most detailed and best-written telling of Aeneas's quest to find a new homeland is the *Aeneid*, an epic poem by the great Roman writer Virgil. He composed it between 29 and 19 BCE, intending to celebrate Rome's many triumphs over the centuries. His secondary motive in writing it was to glorify the image of his friend, Augustus, the first Roman emperor. One inescapable overall theme of the *Aeneid* is that Rome had a divinely ordained destiny to rule the world. In the words of the late expert on ancient Rome, R.H. Barrow:

> The most significant movement of history . . . according to Virgil, is the march of the Roman along the road of his destiny to a high civilization. For in that destiny is to be found the valid and permanent interpretation of all [human] movement and all development. . . . The stately *Aeneid* progresses throughout its length to this theme, the universal and the ultimate triumph of the Roman spirit as the highest manifestation of man's powers.

R.H. Barrow. *The Romans*. New York: Pelican, 1987, pp. 85–86.

ceedingly noble people—the Romans. For them, Jupiter murmured, "I see no measure nor date, and I grant them dominion without end . . . the master race, the wearers of the toga. So it is willed!"[29]

For the later Romans, these words by Jupiter were prophetic and crucial. They accepted Aeneas's mythical exploits as real events and to them his journey seemed to be the most consequential quest in all of mythology. They were well aware of Jason's search for the Golden Fleece and other Greek tales of epic quests, for instance. But those stories ended up with the lead character acquiring merely a single object. In Aeneas's case, in contrast, the Romans felt that the outcome of the quest was much broader in scope. In their view, Aeneas had set in motion Rome's rise to greatness, which had made it possible for that city and its people to rule large portions of the known world. Such was the power of certain selective myths for the Romans and in similar situations for other ancient peoples.

CHAPTER FOUR

Stories of Monster Slayers

The dim-witted demon Keshi slowly crawled through the underbrush lining a big, flower-covered meadow. The stench from his decaying flesh was so overpowering that the area's resident chipmunks, bees, ants, and even worms in the dirt beneath him speedily retreated in utter disgust. Having the appearance of a large, badly deformed horse with a mouthful of crooked teeth, he peeked through some blades of tall grass and caught sight of his intended target. It was an extremely handsome young man who was tossing a ball back and forth among some farm maidens.

Several weeks before, Kamsa, the corrupt ruler of the kingdom in which this scene took place, had summoned Keshi and offered him some gold trinkets in exchange for doing a job for him. That task was to find and kill a young man named Krishna. The latter, the king explained, was a notorious do-gooder who posed a threat to Kamsa's power. Hence, Keshi should quietly and efficiently eliminate him.

Because the demon was not very bright, he had taken a while to find Krishna. And now that his prey was in sight, Keshi was eager to launch his attack. Afterward, not only would the assassin be able to collect the gold the king had promised, he would have a tasty bonus—devouring his victim's remains.

What Keshi did not know was that the young man he was about to assault was no ordinary human being. Krishna was an avatar—a disguised version—of one of the strongest Hindu gods, Vishnu. A highly skilled warrior, as well as a renowned dancer and lover, Krishna was also known for being an avid demon slayer.

Ignorant of his target's formidable abilities, Keshi suddenly leaped up and galloped at top speed toward Krishna. Seeing the creature coming, the young women quickly bolted away in all directions, but their friend was unmoved. Quite clearly unphased by the situation, Krishna grinned, then maneuvered in such a way as to trip his attacker and send him flying face-first onto the ground.

Astounded and outraged, the demon jumped up and again hurled himself at the young man. This time Keshi opened his huge mouth wide in an attempt to swallow his target in one big gulp, yet Krishna remained calm. With amazing swiftness, the young man extended one arm right into the demon's mouth and then, with equally blinding speed, expanded the limb's size, causing Keshi's head to explode with a sickening pop. A second later, the creature's lifeless body dropped down into the blood-covered grass. Finally, acting as if nothing unusual had occurred, Krishna yawned, picked up the ball, and trotted away to find his friends.

Monsters and Heroes from a Remote Era

The often-cited, gory encounter between Krishna and the horse demon is a classic example of one of the most popular themes explored in the world's mythologies: good versus evil. Tales of valiant and heroic monster slayers have for centuries captured people's imaginations. Whether they read those stories in books or see them dramatized in movies, television shows, or video games, people of all walks of life find them endlessly entertaining. They typically involve a hero whose deeds, Oxford University scholar David A. Leeming says, "are at once extraordinary labors and . . . well beyond what we think of as possible."[30] Among those fantastic labors, none are more graphic and exciting as dispatching monsters, which have included demons like Keshi, lions, giants, witches, sea serpents, shape-shifters, and numerous others.

In order to defeat the demon Keshi, Krishna extended one arm into its mouth, as pictured here, and then expanded the arm's size, causing Keshi's head to explode.

The many myths about monster slayers are most often set in a remote past era when supernatural characters, including gods and monsters, were thought to have commonly walked the earth. The ancient Greeks called that dimly remembered era the Age of Heroes. Similarly, the ancient Persians, who dwelled in what is now Iran, also believed that such a bygone heroic age had existed. Long before the Persian Empire arose in the 500s BCE, they believe, the sole god and supreme being (whom they called Ahura Mazda) had created the universe. Not long after that, supposedly an evil being named Angra Mainyu defied God and at the same time brought lies, disorder, and monstrous creatures into the world. In order to counter those bad forces, including the monsters, Ahura Mazda ensured that a number of fearless heroes arose.

The most commendable of those long-ago heroes, the Persians believed, was the muscular and daring Rustam. It was said that he was born with supernatural strength, so much so that even as a small child, he could lift an elephant above his head. He was best known for his battle with the infamous monster Div-e-Sepid, often called the White Demon. With the aid of several thousand evil and hideous henchmen, Div-e-Sepid long controlled the expansive region lying between Iran and the Caspian Sea.

Determined to rid the world of those despicable creatures, Rustam armed himself with an array of weapons. After learning of the location of the cave in the wilderness where Div-e-Sepid lived, the young hero stood near the cave's mouth and challenged the monster to come out and fight. Div-e-Sepid did so, and the bloody bout lasted for hours. In the end, Rustam sliced off the creature's limbs and punctured his liver, after which the monster's cowardly followers ran away and scattered to parts unknown.

A Series of Unnatural and Grisly Murders

Many miles to the northwest of Iran lies Germany. Like the ancient Persians, the ancient Germans had a rich tradition of myths, including several dealing with heroes who rid the world of dangerous monsters. Thanks to an anonymous tenth-century Old English epic poem, *Beowulf*, one of the most important Germanic heroic tales has survived.

The star of the story is the title character, Beowulf. A skilled and stalwart warrior from the kingdom of Geatsland (in what is now Sweden), he heard that the realm of Hrothgar, a noble Danish king, had been suffering a series of attacks by a huge monster. Time after time, that ruler's mead hall (a large communal building for meetings and feasting) had been raided by a creature called Grendel.

Reportedly taller than any human, covered in thick dark fur, and sporting huge, sharp teeth, the beast had several times captured local men and women and eaten them alive. The original poem describes one such episode. Late at night, it says, while a local soldier slept in the mead hall, Grendel appeared and "suddenly tore him [apart]." The monster "bit [through] his bone[s], drank the blood in currents, [and] swallowed [the flesh in] mouthfuls. He soon had the dead man's feet and hands, too, eaten entirely."[31]

Hearing of this series of grisly murders, Beowulf felt compelled to help King Hrothgar and his afflicted people by ridding them of the heinous Grendel. After a long journey, the young man reached Hrothgar's castle, where the king himself heartily welcomed him. That night, accompanied by a few of the king's soldiers, Beowulf went to the empty mead hall and quietly waited in hopes of encountering the evil creature. Sure enough, it appeared. It reached for one of the soldiers but was surprised when a hand suddenly shot forward out of the darkness and tightly grasped the creature's massive wrist. Grendel instinctively tried to pull away, but the hand's grip was incredibly strong. That hand, of course, belonged to Beowulf, who now bore down even harder and dislocated several of the beast's finger joints.

Screaming in pain, Grendel pulled back with all his might in an effort to flee, but the emboldened man tackled him. Grabbing one of the monster's arms, Beowulf twisted with tremendous force, and the sound of a bone snapping reverberated across the hall.

Slaying the Foul Chimaera

Among the most renowned monster-slayers in the annals of world mythology was a Greek hero named Bellerophon. In the words of the second-century CE Greek myth teller today known as Pseudo-Apollodorus, the scary beast he fought, the Chimaera, was "a single being that had the force of three beasts, the front part of a lion, the tail of a dragon, and the third (middle) head was that of a goat, through which it breathed out fire."

The creature terrorized several areas of the Greek-speaking world, especially the region of Lycia (in what is now Turkey). The Lycian ruler, Iobates, had heard about Bellerophon's success in fighting pirates and other criminals. So the king requested that the young man try to slay the Chimaera. Accepting the challenge, Bellerophon mounted the famous flying horse Pegasus, which he had recently captured and tamed. The hero and horse soon found the monster and immediately assaulted it. Although the creature did its best to fight back, it could not evade Pegasus's agile aerial twists and turns and quickly grew tired and fell to the ground. Then Bellerophon dispatched it with his sword. It was said that for centuries afterward that nothing grew in the spot where the foul creature expired.

Pseudo-Apollodorus, *Bibliotheca*, trans. Keith Aldrich, quoted in Theoi Greek Mythology, "Chimaera." www.theoi.com.

Grendel, pictured here, was a creature taller than a human and covered in thick, dark fur, who captured men and women and ate them alive.

With the creature pinned down and writhing in agony, the soldiers rushed forward, swords drawn, and all of them stabbed Grendel repeatedly until his huge body lay lifeless. For his contribution to the monster's demise, Beowulf's name became synonymous with heroism throughout northern Europe.

By Far the Ugliest of All

Germany, the Scandinavian realms, and other parts of northern Europe long commemorated the deeds of some other local monster slayers besides Beowulf. Yet in sheer numbers of such heroes, no European region came close to matching ancient Greece. A few of the numerous famous Greek monster slayers included Theseus (who killed the half-man, half-bull beast known as the Minotaur); Bellerophon (who slew the Chimaera); and Heracles (who eliminated a marauding lion, a giant boar, a herd of flesh-eating horses, and numerous others).

The Challenge of Portraying Medusa in Art

Both literary and archaeological evidence indicates that the ancient Greeks regarded the horrifying character Medusa as the most popular monster and villain in their collected myths. The classic tale of her death at the hands of the hero Perseus was therefore a favorite of storytellers and artists alike. Yet depicting her in artistic renditions such as paintings and sculptures was a decidedly difficult task. This was because of the high degree of evil, danger, and physical damage associated with her. So horrendous was the threat she posed that artists were often at a loss as to how to portray her image. In the words of the late, great scholar of Greek civilization C.M. Bowra:

> Monsters in general depend for their horror on being vague and dimly conceived and are usually ineffective in any art form that insists on making them realistic. Such a creature as the Gorgon Medusa, which was believed to turn men into stone by its mere look, can never be adequately portrayed by human hands, and though Greek Gorgons indeed make ugly grimaces [in paintings and sculptures], they hardly freeze the blood.

C.M. Bowra, *The Greek Experience*. New York: Barnes & Noble, 1996, p. 163.

Arguably the most renowned Greek creature killer, however, was Perseus. His great reputation is based less on his own abilities as a warrior and more on whom he slew. Known as Medusa, over the centuries she was, and remains today, very possibly the most famous of all the world's many mythical monsters. A truly unforgettable character, she was one of three hideous sisters called the Gorgons. According to the ancient Greek writer today called Pseudo-Apollodorus, "they had big tusks like hogs, bronze hands, and wings of gold on which they flew."[32] Medusa was by far the ugliest of all, so much so that anyone whose eyes met hers was turned to stone.

As for Perseus himself, he was semidivine, since his father was the chief Greek god, Zeus, and his mother a mortal woman. Mainly because of his relation to Zeus, people expected him to be a formidable fighter. So one day a local Greek king recruited Perseus to track down and kill the infamous Medusa. Like everyone else, Perseus had heard that she dwelled on a remote island and that she had turned numerous travelers who had ventured onto that island into stone statues.

Light Versus Darkness

Intending to avoid that awful fate, Perseus searched for a way to kill his prey without looking directly at her. Luckily for him, two sympathetic deities decided to help out. Athena, goddess of war, lent Perseus her shield that she had polished until it was highly reflective. Instead of looking directly at Medusa, Athena

Perseus used Hermes's cap to sneak up on Medusa while she was sleeping and cut off her head, as pictured here.

told Perseus, view her only via her reflection in the shield, a trick that would render her lethal gaze harmless.

The second deity who offered Perseus aid was Hermes, messenger of the gods. The latter drew the young man a map that showed the location of the Gorgons' island. Hermes also gifted him a cap that made anyone who wore it invisible and some special sandals that allowed him to fly to the island, which Perseus wasted no time in doing. From high above, he beheld a scary sight. "No matter where he turned," the Roman myth teller Ovid wrote, "he saw both man and beast turned into stone, all creatures who had seen Medusa's face."[33]

Zooming downward, Perseus found Medusa fast asleep on a big, flat rock near the sea. As Athena had instructed, the young man was careful to look at the creature only by reflection. When he positioned himself directly above Medusa, she abruptly woke up and glanced around with a worried expression, as if she could somehow sense his presence. Thanks to Hermes's cap, however, she was unable see her stalker lining up his sword close to her neck. Sure enough, with a swift, well-aimed swing, he decapitated her, and her repulsive body dropped down on the rock with a sickening thud. Meanwhile, Perseus caught the head in a sack, intending to employ it as proof that he had successfully completed his mission.

Perseus and Medusa are fictional characters, as are Rustam, Div-e-Sepid, Beowulf, Grendel, and the rest of the world's mythical monsters and the bigger-than-life heroes who slew them. They are symbols that storytellers used to illustrate the moral concepts of good and evil. Moreover, those age-old ideas were often further represented by the very real phenomena of light and darkness. As modern mythologist Bernard Evslin suggests, such tales "are drenched in sunlight," therein seen as "a moral quality," whereas the evil monsters hide in or retreat into the darkness. Therefore, Evslin continues, "we see a great religious theme—the eternal struggle between the powers of light and the powers of darkness embodied in these simple stories in a way that has branded itself on the human consciousness forever."[34]

CHAPTER FIVE

Stories of Love and Lovers

One day a very long time ago on the Big Island of Hawaii, the sun was shining brightly, and Pele, the Hawaiian goddess of fire and volcanoes, felt it was a perfect day for a walk in the woods. She took her time, stopping frequently along the well-worn path to admire the several picturesque waterfalls. Eventually, as she rounded a bend in the path, Pele caught sight of a man she was certain she had never seen before. Apparently out hunting for small game, he was quite handsome, and within the space of a few minutes the goddess had fallen in love.

Walking to the man, Pele asked him his name, and he told her it was Ohia. Pele then identified herself and urged him not to be afraid. She was a divine, immortal being, to be sure, she said. But she was capable of taking human form, as she was doing at that moment. And if they married, she promised she would be gentle with him always.

These sudden amorous advances made Ohia very uncomfortable. He was not afraid of meeting a goddess; what bothered him was that he had heard Pele was fickle and untrustworthy and had a terrible temper. Moreover, he already had a romantic bond with a woman, a girlfriend named Lehua. He now proceeded to tell Pele that he was already taken and therefore must politely refuse her offer of marriage.

Most human women, and even most goddesses, would have been understanding and wished the young man luck with his present relationship. But just as Ohia had surmised, Pele did indeed have an awful temper. And she interpreted his rejection as a major insult. Furious, she exploded in a fit of anger and let loose some of her formidable supernatural powers. Within mere seconds, she had transformed the unfortunate man into a tree.

When the beautiful maiden Lehua heard what had happened, she was heartbroken. She pleaded with Pele to change poor Ohia back, but the goddess steadfastly refused. At that point, as Lehua wept, several of her ancestors, who were now minor deities, appeared before her. They lacked the power to bring back her beloved, they said. However, they could ensure that the two lovers would be together eternally. With Lehua's permission, they

This mural on the Big Island of Hawaii depicts Pele, the Hawaiian goddess of fire and volcanoes.

transformed her into a magnificent flower on the Ohia tree. That is why modern Hawaiians say one should never pick the flowers of the Ohia tree for doing so might cause the lovers to be separated.

Timeless and Universal Romances

Mythologies of peoples around the world contain such tales of love and lovers. This is hardly surprising when one considers that love is widely viewed as one of the most prevailing and strongest human emotions. It is also the primary basis for family and sibling relationships, marriage, and the creation of new families. For many people love is what makes life worth living.

The ancient Hawaiian tale of the lovers Ohia and Lehua is therefore far from unusual in the world's collected myths. The ancient Egyptians, Greeks, Romans, Chinese, Hindus, Native Americans, and numerous others all had stories that celebrated the beauty and purity of love between spouses, parents and children, siblings, and friends. Moreover, these tales usually involve gods and goddesses said to have overseen the process of love. Such romances are timeless and universal, says modern Egyptian writer Alia El Saady. Reflecting on these stories, she points out, allows people everywhere to realize how love can "transform itself, not only into different kinds but different tales as well, and cross culturally and across different timelines . . . cultures, religions, and histories."[35]

To appreciate just how pervasive such tales of love have been in the past, one need look no further than the classic Chinese love story of Niu Lang and Zhi Nu. This myth is set in the extremely distant past, when the entire cosmos was quite young. Back then, according to ancient Chinese sources, each of the brightest stars in the sky was occupied by a minor deity. Zhi Nu inhabited the feminine star that Westerners call Vega, and Niu Lang lived within the masculine star called Altair.

After the passage of several years, the two celestial beings got to know each other and fell in love. Unfortunately for them, however, they were forced to keep their mutual feelings a secret be-

Reunited After Twenty Years

Another famous ancient Greek tale of powerful romantic love is the myth of Odysseus and his wife Penelope. Their personal love story is part of the larger myth told by the renowned ancient Greek epic poet Homer in his immortal work the *Odyssey*. Odysseus, ruler of the Greek island kingdom of Ithaca, met Penelope and the two fell deeply in love, married, and had a son named Telemachus. When the boy was still quite young, Odysseus accompanied other Greek kings in the famous ten-year siege of Troy. When the war ended, Odysseus intended to return to his beloved wife and son. But his ships got lost in a great storm, and for ten more years he wandered among strange unknown lands. Meanwhile, in Ithaca, where most people assumed Odysseus had died, Penelope was beset by dozens of suitors, demanding she marry one of them. Fortunately for her, her husband eventually made it home, slew the suitors, and heartily embraced her. On their first night together in twenty years, the sympathetic goddess Athena delayed the coming of the dawn so that their joyous reunion would be extended.

cause the powerful goddess who controlled the sky—the Queen of the West—did not like the beings she ruled expressing romantic feelings for one another.

Eventually, the queen did discover the lovers' secret and decided to punish them. First, she transformed Zhi Nu into a cloud weaver, a minor nature spirit who caused clouds to form pleasant-looking patterns in the sky. Worse, the queen turned Niu Lang into a lowly human cowherd in a small village on earth.

The Cow's Secret

Niu and Zhi were, not surprisingly, emotionally crushed by these events. Miserable over their forced separation, Niu stopped smiling and Zhi cried every night. Even so, neither one lost hope that that they would see each other again someday.

That hope finally came to fruition, because several years later the queen allowed Zhi Nu to visit earth. The despondent cloud weaver was able to go swimming in a pond in a lovely, tree-lined park. Meanwhile, at that particular time Niu Lang was poverty stricken. The only things he owned were an aging cow and an old wooden wagon. The man and cow dwelled together in a tiny, rickety shack. And one day the cow told Niu, "Today you shall go to a beautiful park. There you will see angels bathing."[36] And there, the cow went on, the man would meet his future wife.

Intrigued, Niu did as the cow proposed and traveled to the park. There he saw the young woman swimming and immediately recognized his lost love, Zhi. Together again, they wasted no time in getting married. And in the years that followed, they and the cow lived in a small house Niu constructed himself.

In the myth of Niu Lang and Zhi Nu, the Queen of the West, pictured here, did not like that the lovers had feelings for one another.

Eventually, the cow died. Seconds before passing away, it told Niu a secret it had long kept from him. Many years before, the creature explained, it too had been a star in the sky, and the queen had punished it by turning it into an earthly cow. While marooned on earth, it had decided to always protect its former fellow star spirits—Niu and Zhi. In the centuries following the cow's death, Niu and Zhi were inseparable, and they never forgot their bovine friend.

All of Nature's Residents Wept

Over the centuries, most people in China came to agree that the feelings Niu and Zhi shared were an example of pure, true love. Examples of that same widely coveted emotion appear in ancient Greek mythology as well. One is the story of the ill-fated couple Orpheus and Eurydice. A courageous soldier and skilled musician, Orpheus was known for writing sad love songs so moving that all of the natural world became entranced by them. "Even trees and stones were believed to come and hear his music,"[37] historians Michael Grant and John Hazel remark.

Females of all species were especially spellbound by Orpheus's songs. One of their number was the nymph Eurydice. This minor nature goddess became so captivated by the young musician that she soon fell in love with him. It did not take him long to reciprocate that feeling, and thereafter he composed many new love songs for her. Moreover, only months after their first meeting, they married.

The two were fortunate enough to enjoy several years of happy marriage together. And then one day Eurydice suffered a bite by a poisonous snake and died. Overcome by intense grief, Orpheus wracked his brain trying to think of a way to somehow reverse the situation and get his beloved wife back. His friends claimed such a thing was impossible. No one, they pointed out, could induce the powerful king of the underworld, Hades, to give up a soul he had already brought to his shadowy subterranean abode.

So much did Orpheus pine for his lost love that he rejected that advice. Determined to retrieve his wife, he decided to risk everything by descending into the dark depths and confronting Hades himself. Swords and other weapons would be useless against a god, he realized. But he was confident of another sort of powerful device he had mastered. He would use his music to manipulate the denizens of the world of the dead.

Sure enough, when Orpheus eventually made it to Hades's dimly lit palace and sang for the lord of the dead, the many grim-looking creatures guarding the king began to cry. Even Hades wept aloud. Moreover, the dark lord relented and, as Grant and Hazel write, granted Orpheus "a favor, allowing him to recover Eurydice on one condition. He must lead the way and not look back at her until they reached the upper air again."[38]

Overcome with joy, Orpheus led his wife upward through the murky tunnels. Mile after mile, he carefully adhered to the condition imposed by Hades. He refrained from looking back at

The Maiden and the Fish-Man

Many Native American tribes have myths about love. One told and retold by the Sioux, a Great Plains people, begins with a young hunter approaching a beautiful young maiden and asking her to marry him. He professes love for her, and she does the same in return. However, she explains, her father will not sanction the union unless the young suitor performs a brave deed that the entire tribe can celebrate. The suitor agrees to do his best and leaves the village with a few of his friends. They go in search of some sort of adventure that will allow the young man to perform a noteworthy deed. Eventually, they see a strange mound beside a river and climb atop it. It turns out to be not a mound but the back of a giant turtle. It attacks the young men and most of them die trying to fight it. As for the suitor, he turns into a large fish and starts living in the river. On hearing about these events, the young maiden travels to the river and confronts the fish-man. They agree that although they still love each other, they cannot have a life together, and they part from each other in abject sadness. For the Sioux, this story was a reminder that not all male-female relationships are fated to work out.

While leading Eurydice out of the underworld, Orpheus turned to look back for a fraction of a second, as shown here, and she was immediately lost to him.

Eurydice. Only a few seconds before they reached the surface, however, the urge to see her became too much for him, and he peeked back for a fraction of a second. At that instant, Ovid recalled, Eurydice shrank backward with enormous force. Desperately, "Orpheus stretched out his arms, straining to clasp her, but the hapless man touched nothing but yielding air. [Crying out] a last farewell which scarcely reached his ears, she fell back [into the abyss].[39]

The Stable Boy and the Boss's Daughter

The tragedy of Orpheus and Eurydice is matched in sadness and intensity by few other love stories in the annals of world mythology. One of them, modern mythologists agree, is a classic tragic romance from ancient India. It is the story of Heer and Ranjha.

The youngest of eight brothers, Ranjha was a happy-go-lucky youth who spent most of his time playing his flute. The young man's life altered dramatically, however, when his father died. His seven brothers viewed him as a useless dreamer and refused to give him his fair share of the money the father had left behind. Dejected, Ranjha left town and traveled to a distant region of India. There he got a job as a stable boy, and before long he had fallen deeply in love with his boss's daughter. Her name was Heer, and she soon informed Ranjha that she was profoundly in love with him as well. Because the two knew that her wealthy father would disapprove of her being with a stable boy, they resolved to keep their relationship a secret.

A few months later, however, the father did find out. He insisted that the two young people never see each other again. Heer's parents also forced her to marry a man she had never met. Furious and heartbroken, Ranjha ran off into a nearby wilderness area, became a Hindu monk, and adopted a lifestyle in which he survived by begging for food.

About a year later, the young man approached a house in hopes of obtaining some food and discovered it was the home where Heer and her husband dwelled. When the two former lovers recognized each other, they could not help but rekindle their mutual passion, and they daringly escaped to a neighboring town. Fortunately for them, a sympathetic local official took their side. He dissolved Heer's first marriage, which allowed her to marry Ranjha. But a happy ending for the couple was not to be. Heer's parents were so enraged by this turn of events that they poisoned the newlyweds, who died in each other's arms.

Stories of this sort inevitably touch the hearts and souls of people in all cultures around the globe. "What distinguishes average love stories from the great?" asks Texas-based storyteller Sandhya Raghavan. Her answer is their tragic endings, "usually, the untimely death of the star-crossed lovers . . . and that's exactly what made sagas like Heer-Ranjha [and] Romeo-Juliet stand the test of time [and become widely viewed] as the golden standard for true love."[40]

SOURCE NOTES

Introduction: Universal Tales That Explore Life's Meaning

1. Reading Is Fundamental, "Myths and Legends from Around the World." https://earth.google.com.
2. Michael Grant and John Hazel, *Who's Who in Classical Mythology*. London: Routledge, 2004, p. vii.
3. Grant and Hazel, *Who's Who in Classical Mythology*, pp. vii–viii.
4. Joshua J. Mark, "Mythology," World History Encyclopedia, October 31, 2018. www.worldhistory.org.
5. Mark, "Mythology."

Chapter One: Stories of Creation

6. Quoted in Caroline Seawright, "Khnum, Potter God of the Inundation Silt and Creation," Tour Egypt. www.touregypt.net.
7. Robert L. Carneiro, "Origin Myths," National Center for Science Education, November 3, 2008. https://ncse.ngo.
8. W.H.D. Rouse, *Gods, Heroes and Men of Ancient Greece*. New York: New American Library, 2001, p. 11.
9. Ovid, *Metamorphoses*," trans. Horace Gregory. New York: New American Library, 1958, pp. 31–32.
10. Shen Yun Performing Arts, "Mythistory Begins," August 24, 2016. www.shenyunperformingarts.org.
11. Shen Yun Performing Arts, "Mythistory Begins."
12. Quoted in Miguel Leon-Portilla, *Aztec Thought and Culture: A Study of the Ancient Nahuatl Mind*. Norman: University of Oklahoma Press, 1990, p. 90.
13. H.W.F. Saggs. *Babylonians*. Berkeley: University of California Press, 2000, p. 32.

Chapter Two: Stories of Warring Gods

14. Quoted in Joshua J. Mark, "Enuma Elish—the Babylonian Epic of Creation—Full Text," World History Encyclopedia, May 4, 2018. www.worldhistory.org.
15. Quoted in Mark, "Enuma Elish."
16. Quoted in Mark, "Enuma Elish."
17. Shashank, "Top 10 Deadly Fights from Different Mythologies," Gobookmart, February 27, 2023. https://gobookmart.com.

18. Quoted in Shahrukh Husain, *Demons, Gods, and Holy Men from Indian Myths and Legends*. New York: Bedrick, 1987, p. 71.
19. Quoted in Husain, *Demons, Gods, and Holy Men from Indian Myths and Legends*, p. 71.
20. Quoted in Hari P. Shastri, trans., *Ramayana*, ed. Elizabeth Seeger. New York: Scott, 1969, pp. 212–13.
21. Quoted in Philip Vellacott, trans., *Aeschylus: Prometheus Bound, The Suppliants, Seven Against Thebes, The Persians*. Baltimore, MD: Penguin, 1961, p. 27.
22. Quoted in H.G. Evelyn-White, trans., *Hesiod, the Homeric Hymns, and Homerica*. Cambridge, MA: Harvard University Press, 1964, pp. 129, 131.
23. Edith Hamilton, *Mythology*. New York: Grand Central, 1999, p. 300.
24. Daniel McCoy, "Ragnarok," Norse Mythology for Smart People. https://norse-mythology.org.
25. H.R.E. Davidson, *Scandinavian Mythology*. New York: Bedrick, 1986, p. 218.

Chapter Three: Stories of Epic Quests

26. Quoted in Stephanie Dalley, trans., *Myths from Mesopotamia*. New York: Oxford University Press, 1989, pp. 92–93.
27. Quoted in Virgil, *Aeneid*, trans. Patric Dickinson. New York: New American Library, 1961, pp. 57–58.
28. Quoted in Virgil, *Aeneid*, pp. 172–73.
29. Quoted in Virgil, *Aeneid*, p. 14.

Chapter Four: Stories of Monster Slayers

30. David A. Leeming, "The Hero," Oxford Academic, 2022. https://academic.oup.com.
31. John L. Hall, trans., *Beowulf*, Chapter 12, "Grendel and Beowulf," Standard Books. https://standardebooks.org.
32. Quoted in Theoi Greek Mythology, "Gorgons and Medusa." www.theoi.com.
33. Ovid, *Metamorphoses*, trans. Rolfe Humphries. Bloomington: Indiana University Press, 1967, p. 134.
34. Bernard Evslin, *Heroes, Gods and Monsters of the Greek Myths*. New York: Laurel Leaf, 1984, p. x.

Chapter Five: Stories of Love and Lovers

35. Alia El Saady, "Myths and Legends of Love," *Identity*, February 26, 2017. https://identity-mag.com.

36. Quoted in World Stories, "The Story of Niu Lang and Zhi Nu." https://worldstories.org.uk.

37. Grant and Hazel, *Who's Who in Classical Mythology*, p. 250.

38. Grant and Hazel, *Who's Who in Classical Mythology*, p. 250.

39. Ovid, *Metamorphoses*, trans. Mary M. Innes. London: Penguin, 2006, p. 226.

40. Sandhya Raghavan, "Do Tragic Love Stories like Romeo and Juliet Influence Our Idea of Love?," Health Site, February 14, 2018. www.thehealthsite.com.

FOR FURTHER RESEARCH

Books

Paul Collins, *The Sumerians*. London: Reaktion, 2021.

Bernard Evslin, *Bernard Evslin's Greek Mythology*. Los Angeles: Graymalkin, 2023.

Neil Gaiman, *Norse Mythology*, vols. 1–3. Milwaukie, OR: Dark Horse, 2021.

Michael Grant and John Hazel, *Who's Who in Classical Mythology*. London: Routledge, 2002.

Vatsala Sperling, *Classic Tales from India*. Rochester, VT: Bear Club, 2020.

Jiankun Sun, *Fantastic Creatures of the Mountains and Seas: A Chinese Classic*. New York: Arcade, 2021.

Billy Wellman, *Egyptian History and Mythology*. Self-published, 2022.

Internet Sources

Michael Butcher, "Krishna," Mythopedia, May 19, 2023. https://mythopedia.com.

Guillaume Deprez, "Goddess Isis: Fascinating Facts About the Mother of All Gods," The Collector, April 24, 2021. www.thecollector.com.

Ducksters, "Greek Mythology: The Titans." www.ducksters.com.

Glencairn Museum, "Ancient Egyptian Creation Myths: From Watery Chaos to Cosmic Egg," July 13, 2021. www.glencairnmuseum.org.

Greeka, "Jason and the Argonauts," 2023. www.greeka.com.

Mae Hamilton, "Pangu," Mythopedia, December 1, 2022. https://mythopedia.com.

Pace University, "The History Behind Beowulf." https://csis.pace.edu.

Ansel Pereira, "100 Most Powerful Gods and Goddesses of War," Owlcation, June 15, 2021. https://owlcation.com.

Rick Riordan, "Meet the Egyptian Gods," Rick Riordan personal website. http://rickriordan.com.

Jess Scott, "A Beginner's Guide to Norse Mythology," Life in Norway, December 3, 2020. www.lifeinnorway.net.

Swedish History Museum, "Odin: The One-Eyed All-Father." https://historiska.se.

World Stories, "The Story of Niu Lang and Zhi Nu." https://worldstories.org.uk.

Websites

Ancient Egypt Site

www.ancient-egypt.org
Belgian Egyptologist Jacques Kinnaer writes and updates the text of the many pages of this colorful presentation of ancient Egyptian history and culture.

Aztec Gods—Who's Who?, Aztec History

www.aztec-history.com/aztec-gods.html
Mexican researcher Jamie Cottrill gives colorfully illustrated summaries of five of the major Aztec gods.

Indian Mythological Stories, KidsGen

www.kidsgen.com/fables_and_fairytales/indian_mythology_stories
This useful site contains links to dozens of individual ancient Indian myths, along with colorful pictures of various characters from those stories.

Norse Mythology for Smart People

https://norse-mythology.org
Written by David McCoy, a noted scholar of Norse myths and folklore, this site contains a rounded, detailed look at the Norse myths. It provides numerous links to supportive articles, including ones on the various Norse gods, Norse cosmology, Viking culture, and diverse Norse writings.

Theoi Greek Mythology

www.theoi.com
This is the most comprehensive and reliable general website about Greek mythology on the internet. It features hundreds of separate pages filled with detailed, accurate information, as well as numerous primary sources and reproductions of ancient paintings and mosaics.

PICTURE CREDITS

ABOUT THE AUTHOR

Classical historian and award-winning author Don Nardo has written numerous acclaimed volumes about ancient civilizations and peoples. They include more than fifty overviews of the mythologies of the Sumerians, Babylonians, Egyptians, Greeks, Romans, Persians, Celts, Hindus, Native Americans, and others. Nardo, who also composes and arranges orchestral music, lives with his wife, Christine, in Massachusetts.